Arctic
Adve

Written by Adam and Charlotte Guillain

Essex County Council

3013021573424 4

It was an exciting day at the wildlife park.

"Some little owl chicks have hatched!" Tess and Finn's mum told them. "Can you help me get their new cage ready?"

As Tess and Finn swept out the new cage, an icy wind whistled across the park.

The wind blew a white feather through the air. As Tess caught it, she and Finn were swept away!

"Where are we?" gasped Tess. They had landed in thick white snow that glistened in the sunlight.

"It looks like the Arctic," said Finn. "We watched a documentary about it last week!"

Tess trudged across the snow to explore but Finn called her back.

"What's that?" he asked, pointing to something on the ground.

Tess looked back and cried, "It's a nest! There are snowy owl chicks inside!"

She ran to the nest and sank to her knees.

"Where's your mum?" she asked the chicks.

The baby owls shivered as the cold wind blew their feathers.

"She went to find food," squeaked one owl. "We're so hungry."

"I want her to come back," wailed the other chick.

Tess looked around. There was no sign of the mother owl, and it was starting to snow.

"We'll go and search for her," said Finn. "Try to stay warm!"

Tess and Finn set off. The snow blew all around them, like they were in a snow globe.

"I don't know how we'll find her," shouted Tess. "I can't see anything!"

Finn thought they would have to turn back.
But then he heard something.

Screech!

"Listen!" cried Finn. "What's that sound?"

Screech!

"There it is again!" shouted Finn.

Which direction is it coming from?

Tess stared through the swirling snow.

"Over there!" she cried and they ran to a shape on the ground.

"The mother owl!" gasped Finn.

"My babies!" screeched the mother owl.
"Have you seen them? Are they all right?"

"Yes," said Tess. "They're fine, but
they're hungry!"

The sad mother owl screeched weakly.

"I've been searching for food for so long. I'm too tired to fly any more. It's impossible to find food in this weather."

Tess held out her arm.

"We'll take you back to your nest," she said.

The mother owl hopped on to Tess's glove.

"Which way is it?" Finn asked her.

The owl nodded her head to show the way. Soon they could hear the cries of the baby owls.

"Something's wrong!" said their mother.

"It's a fox!" yelled Tess.

Finn ran towards the nest, waving his arms and shouting. The fox leaped in the air and scampered away.

"Thank you," said the mother owl. She hopped from Tess's glove into the nest.

The chicks snuggled up to their mother.

"I'll keep you safe and warm until I can hunt again," she told them.

"I think the snow is stopping!" said Tess.

As the snow stopped falling, the sun came out. It lit up the icy ground. The twins' feet slipped about on the ice.

"I think we're going back!" shouted Finn. "Goodbye!"

Back at the wildlife park, Mum was at the little owls' cage. "They look safe and happy now," she said.

"Just like the snowy owls in the Arctic!"
Tess whispered to Finn.

Talk about the story

Answer the questions:

1 What was inside the nest that Finn spots?

2 What was the mother owl busy doing?

3 Why were the chicks shivering?

4 Why did Tess carry the mother owl back
to the nest?

5 What do you think the fox was doing near the nest?

6 Have you ever seen baby chicks? What type
of bird were they?

Can you retell the story in your own words?